The Snake in the Ca

Part 5: Fire and Flame

The focus in this book is on the split digraphs

'a-e, i-e, o-e' in the words:

flame   snake   cave   saved

came   side   fire   wide

closer   rose   stone

Wellington went back to his kennel. He sat down. He thought about the big snake. He thought about the sad dragon.

Soon he was dreaming again. In this dream he was going into the cave with a candle. The flame of the candle was lit.

Wellington found the tunnel in the side of the cave. He went down it. He came to the cavern. The sad dragon was on his flat stone.

Wellington put the candle on the floor next to the dragon's sausages. Then he told the dragon to blow over the flame of the candle.

The dragon blew over the candle's flame. His fire was lit. He could breathe flames. He was a proper dragon again.

The dragon was very happy. He had fire. He could breathe out flames again. He could cook his sausages for his dinner.

All of a sudden, the dragon saw a big snake sliding across the floor. It was coming closer and closer to Wellington.

The snake rose up. It hissed. Wellington saw it. The snake opened its mouth wide. Wellington saw its two sharp fangs. Help!

Flames shot past Wellington. The dragon breathed out his fire. The snake moved quickly and the flames just missed it.

The snake was afraid now. It slid away across the floor of the cavern. The dragon had saved Wellington's life.

Vowel graphemes used in this book

ay, ai, a-e:	snake cave again flame came afraid away saved
ee, ea:	dreaming dream breathe
i, i-e:	sliding fire wide life side
o, o-e, ow:	opened over stone told blow closer rose
oo, ew:	soon blew
oo:	cook
ow, ou:	down out about found mouth now
or:	for floor
er:	cavern over proper dinner closer
ar:	sharp